Do You Do It with the Lights On?

ALSO BY MEL PORETZ AND BARRY SINROD

*The First Really Important Survey of
American Habits*

Do You Do It with the Lights On ?

Mel Poretz
and
Barry Sinrod

Fawcett Columbine
New York

A Fawcett Columbine Book
Published by Ballantine Books
Copyright © 1991 by Mel Poretz and Barry Sinrod

All rights reserved under International and Pan-American Copyright Conventions. Published in the United States by Ballantine Books, a division of Random House, Inc., New York, and simultaneously in Canada by Random House of Canada Limited, Toronto.

Library of Congress Catalog Card Number: 91-70534
ISBN: 0-449-90571-3

Cover design by William Geller
Text design by Beth Tondreau Design / Mary A. Wirth

Manufactured in the United States of America
First Edition: October 1991

10 9 8 7 6 5 4

To all my wild, crazy, and very sexy friends. I am dedicating this book to Dr. Alan Chalfin, who was a great friend for more than 20 years. Alan passed away in January 1991 and we miss him very much. Both he and his wife, Eta, spent a great deal of time with us developing the questions for this book. Now, a thank-you to my very special friends for their wit and wisdom and contributions to this book. I've only space to list but a few of the most important names, but all of you know who you are—including Bill, Barbara, Fran, Donna, and Jennifer. Thanks to the gang at Tel-Star USA, especially Allen, for assisting us in the tabulation of all of this wonderful data. Finally, thanks to my wonderful, sexy wife, Shelly, and my children—Marlo, Blake, Jodey—and my son-in-law, David. My current and future grandchildren are too young to read this book, so we will save it for when they are 21!

Barry Sinrod

Anything good that has happened to me since I was 23 is the doing of my wife, Inez, and the great works she produced, our sons Ted and Victor, aided in ample measure recently by their wives, Beth and Meg. I can't begin to thank them in this paragraph.

Mel Poretz

Introduction

HOW NORMAL are you? Do you do the "right" thing? What *is* the right thing when it comes to matters of sex, sleeping, and toilette? We set out to find the norms in these matters with a national survey using a representative sample of households throughout the United States. We covered all 50 states and people from all walks of life.

What we got back were completed and informative questionnaires that were filled out in the privacy of home. The 3,144 replies came from the normal, the not-so-normal, and some quite bizarre people.

Our survey is neither the first nor the last on the subject. It makes no attempt to out-Kinsey Kinsey, to top Ms. Hite, or to trump Masters and Johnson in their specialties. But it does tell us what we (and the world) were waiting to learn. For although Kinsey and his fellow doyens may have established Americans' *exact* sexual frequency, it remained for a couple of graduates of Abraham Lincoln High School in Coney Island to establish definitively Americans' *desires* for sexual frequency.

Do You Do It with the Lights On? will allow you to judge for yourself whether you are normal, a little crazy, or just plain sexy! And no matter how you might twist and squirm, you can't help but recognize yourself in here . . . because our sample represents over 89 percent of the country's adult population and statistically has been proved to be accurate, within a margin of plus-or-minus 3 percent.

Let the data begin:

53 percent of the respondents were male, 47 percent fe-

male. Of the women, 80 percent were employed, 63 percent full-time. 89 percent of the men were employed, 81 percent full-time. 8 percent of our sample were retired.

The average age of the men in our survey was 40.5, spanning a range from 21 to 92. The average age of the women was 38, with the ages ranging from 21 to 86.

Our respondents had, on the average, 2.33 children. Three families in the survey had 6 children, 2 families had 9 children, and 6 families had 10 children.

The average annual income of our respondents was $42,600. 14 percent earned in excess of $100,000, and 9 percent earned less than $15,000. This indicates a very realistic cross section of America.

Educationally, 52 percent had attended or graduated college, and more than 20 percent had postgraduate degrees.

You might be interested to know that 12 percent of the respondents to our survey were left-handed.

Our survey included appropriate proportional representations from many minorities, including Native Americans, Oriental Americans, Hispanic Americans, and African Americans.

For a bit more on demographics, check out the back of the book. Otherwise . . . find out where *you* fit in compared with your fellow Americans by turning the page and beginning your journey.

If you want to share comments with us, or if you have any deep-seated questions you think could be a significant addition to our next survey, send them to us at P.O. BOX 791, JERICHO, N.Y. 11763.

Do You Do It
with the
Lights On?

Do You Enjoy Sex?

	% ALWAYS	% USUALLY	% SOMETIMES
MEN	**75**	**25**	**0**
18–29	67	32	1
30–54	65	34	1
55+	86	14	0
WOMEN	**37**	**55**	**8**
18–29	30	65	5
30–54	38	52	10
55+	44	44	12

Twice as many men as women report that they *always* enjoy sex (75 to 37 percent). And take a look at men and women over 55: the percentage of those who *always* enjoy sex is on the increase. This has got to mean that as you age, sex only gets better and better!

If you look at our chart, you will see that more women than men told us that they *usually* enjoy sex (55 to 25 percent), but that's only because most of the men told us that they *always* enjoy it.

Would you like to know the profile of the scant 37 percent of the women who told us they *always* enjoy sex? To spot her, look for a woman who earns over $25,000 a year, has a college degree, and who doesn't have any kids. Usually she's right-handed, long-haired, tall, and slim.

When You Visit Someone's Home, Do You Look Inside Their Medicine Cabinet?

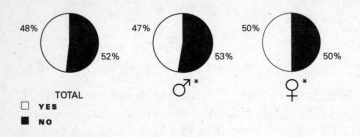

48% 52%
TOTAL

47% 53%
♂*

50% 50%
♀*

☐ YES
■ NO

The answer to this question might encourage you to clean up your own medicine cabinet before you have any more visitors over! Nearly half (48 percent) of us actually admit to having looked into someone's medicine cabinet for no apparent reason other than to snoop.

Since we're speaking of snoops, those who are most likely to venture where they do not belong are college-educated men who earn over $25,000 a year. Sound like anyone you might know?

If you want to play it safe, invite women 55 and over to your home; a resounding 80 percent declare themselves willing to resist the temptation!

* ♂ MALE
♀ FEMALE

How Many Times a Week Do You Have Sex (On Average)?

# OF TIMES:	0	1	2	3	4	5	6	7	8 +	AVG.
% TOTAL SURVEYED	4	26	25	18	10	8	3	4	2	2.74
% MEN	4	30	26	12	9	10	3	1	5	2.52
18–29	6	29	18	23	6	9	1	1	7	2.65
30–54	2	32	26	9	12	9	2	7	1	2.57
55+	7	28	29	7	7	10	10	1	1	2.41
% WOMEN	3	21	25	21	10	5	3	1	11	2.97
18–29	4	19	9	28	14	9	4	4	9	3.33
30–54	6	13	42	13	1	2	6	16	1	2.80
55+	2	24	25	20	12	4	2	4	6	2.75

How Much Sex Is Enough, Is Enough, Is Enough?

See how you rate! Couples, on the average, have sex *2.74* times a week.

The women, though, report making love 2.97 times a week—which is more than the men claim, with 2.52. This means that some women must be having sex alone!

The women who have the most weekly sex earn less than $25,000 a year and have a high-school education. They are likely to have long hair, be right-handed, and have no kids.

The "sexiest" men have a slightly different profile than the "sexiest" women. They earn over $25,000, hold a college degree, and are left-handed. However, like their female counterparts, they also have long hair and no children.

How Many Times a Week Would You Like to Have Sex?

# OF TIMES:	0	1	2	3	4	5	6	7	8 +	AVG.
% TOTAL SURVEYED	1	7	19	18	16	13	4	12	10	5.02
% MEN	0	7	13	15	15	18	5	13	14	5.33
18–29	0	17	0	17	25	17	0	0	24	4.83
30–54	0	5	11	21	21	21	5	16	0	4.21
55 +	1	3	21	10	7	17	7	17	18	6.28
% WOMEN	2	7	25	20	17	9	3	10	7	4.69
18–29	0	13	22	13	17	13	9	9	4	3.96
30–54	5	5	14	29	19	10	0	14	4	5.10
55 +	0	0	47	20	13	0	0	7	13	5.27

Wishing Might Make It So!

When it comes to fantasy, the average goes from an actual *2.74* times a week to a wishful *5.02*. It seems that men wished a little harder, to *5.33*, with the women not far behind at *4.69*.

It took this question in *Do You Do It with the Lights On?* to disprove the old wives' tale that the older you get, the less of a sex drive you have! In our survey, it was the 55 and older set for both genders who indicated the most desire for love-making.

In fact, the profile of those who are wishing for more and more and more is virtually the same among both men and women. *Is this you?* Similarities show that the most fanciful dreamers have a high-school education, earn less than $25,000 a year, and are taller and weigh more than the average. And, yes, they are parents.

Our hope is that theirs—and everyone's—wishes come true!

Do You Close the Bathroom Door When You Are Alone at Home?

	% YES	% NO
MEN	**32**	**68**
18–29	25	75
30–54	25	75
55+	40	60
WOMEN	**18**	**82**
18–29	16	84
30–54	5	95
55+	40	60

Since only 25 percent of Americans close the bathroom door when they are alone at home, the real question becomes, "Why bother with the bathroom door at all?" Most of the door closers reported that they have children who could sneak in at any time, while the door openers, for the most part, did not have any kids. Seems simple enough to us . . . although we *are* surprised by how many women in the 30-to-54 age bracket fearlessly leave that door wide open.

Do You Ever Fantasize About Someone Else During Sex?

	% YES	% NO
MEN	51	49
18–29	61	39
30–54	61	39
55 +	39	61
WOMEN	37	63
18–29	32	68
30–54	33	67
55 +	44	56

Fantasy Love!

Men report fantasizing while having sex to a much larger degree than women, 51 to 37 percent . . . leading us to wonder if that's the reason men are more likely to *always* enjoy sex!

Anyone care to explain why men over 55 have a tendency *not* to dream (only 39 percent, compared with 61 percent for the younger men), while women who reach that same age bracket start fantasizing *more* than their younger counterparts?

The upper-income earners ($25,000+) dream more than the lower-income earners (56 to 44 percent), while those who do not have a college degree fantasize more than those who do (59 to 41 percent).

A few more juicy tidbits: those couples who *do not* have children dream less than those who *do* have children; men who tell us that they are overweight fantasize more than those who are average or underweight; women with short hair fantasize more than those with long hair; and lefties fantasize more than righties!

Who Do You Fantasize About Making Love To?

Get ready for an adventure. The fantasies listed are in rank order of frequency and we've provided the percentage of respondents who made mention of each particular fantasy.

(NOTE: TOTALS ADD UP TO MORE THAN 100 PERCENT DUE TO MULTIPLE FANTASIES!)

FEMALE FANTASIES	PERCENTAGE
Her Best Friend of Opposite Sex	56

To all you men who have a woman as a "best friend": you're in her dreams more often than you think.

Her Boss	25

It's a surprise to us: bosses finished a strong second in the fantasy derby.

Her Teacher	24

Teachers, take note of those good-looking females in your class. Chances are one-in-four they may be taking note of you as well.

Her Garage Mechanic	18

Why do we feel that men may start bringing their cars in for service themselves?!

Her Best Friend's
Husband   15

> Watch out, bosom buddies. There may be an asp in your midst!

Her Doctor   13
Her Accountant   13

> These two pros rank quite far down on the list of nighttime fantasy figures. Could it be because they charge so much for house calls?!

Her Secretary   12

> Male secretaries who work for female employers, beware: you may be in for some special dictation!

Other careers showing up on our survey include:

Her Mailman, Meter
Man, Therapist   6 percent each
Her Gardener   4
Her Golf Pro   3
Her Dentist   1

Don't forget that men have fantasies, too!

His Best Friend of Opposite Sex — 61

Seems that men have even more of an urge in the direction of their best friend of the opposite gender than do women. Are we unintentionally confirming that popular theory that men cannot be friends with women, because they are always thinking about having sex with them?!

His Best Friend's Wife — 39

Men dream about their best friends' wives by more than two to one over the women polled for this category. Interesting!

His Secretary — 37

Few men, married or single, seem able to resist the idea of a liaison with their secretaries.

His Teacher — 36

Seems obvious that men dream of staying after school with their teachers . . . or their children's teachers.

His Nurse — 27

Lots of men put health-care professionals on their list of subjects for nighttime flights of fancy. Does medical insurance cover such nocturnal visits?!

Baby-sitter — 22

It was the men aged 30 to 54 who most fancied a dalliance with visiting teenyboppers.

The list continues:

Best Friend (same sex)	3
Best Friend's Husband	3
Dentist	1
Doctor	1
Therapist	1

Sexual Fantasies with the Stars

We asked participants to tell us what stars they fantasize about, and we were not surprised by the response. However, first we'd like to note a few peculiarities:

More than a few of the respondents admitted to fantasizing about Lassie and Mr. Ed. And an 81-year-old man reported that his movie-star fantasy was June Allyson. We don't know if she turns him on from her days as the star of the 40s musicals, or as a spokeswoman for the adult diapers she currently does commercials for.

The celebrities who were the fantasies for over 10 percent of the population included:

Mel Gibson	Julia Roberts
Patrick Swayze	Jaclyn Smith
Kevin Costner	Demi Moore
Charlie Sheen	Kathleen Turner
Michael Douglas	Kim Basinger
Richard Gere	Jane Fonda
M. C. Hammer	Madonna
Michael Jackson	Janet Jackson
Woody Allen	Erica Kane (Susan Lucci)

Other celebrities that ranked favorably:

Reggie Jackson	Jennifer Capriati
Phil Donahue	Martina Navratilova
Arsenio Hall	Jamie Lee Curtis
Johnny Carson	Janet Leigh
John F. Kennedy, Jr.	Oprah Winfrey
John Goodman	Joan Rivers
Geraldo Rivera	Minnie Pearl
Pee Wee Herman	Elvira
Sam Kinison	Jessica Hahn
Sam Donaldson	Roseanne Barr
Dan Rather	Barbara Bush

Pee Wee Herman? Barbara Bush? What's going on here?!

Have You Ever Used a Public Rest Room Designated for the Opposite Sex?

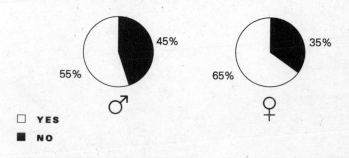

45%

55%

♂

35%

65%

♀

☐ YES
■ NO

When you gotta go, you gotta go! 55 percent of men and 65 percent of women have used a public rest room earmarked for the opposite sex. So the next time you can't wait, remember the precedent set by 60 percent of the American public and *go to it!*

The men and women who have used opposite-sex rest rooms have exactly the same profile: they both had to go when they had to go!

Now, why is it that while only 40 percent of women over 55 have perpetrated this deed, 80 percent of women 30 to 54 have thrown away any and all inhibitions and pushed their way in!

What we can't understand is why 75 percent of men 18 to 29 *needed* to use an opposite-sex facility. Have they forgotten about the macho man and the great outdoors?!

BULLETIN: We wish that we had published this book when a young woman in one of our major cities was actually arrested for using the men's room. We could have come to her defense with the results of this survey. P.S. She was found not guilty!

If You Have a Pet, Do You Let It Stay in the Room When You Are Having Sex?

Among Those Who Let the Pet Stay, Do You Let the Pet Stay on the Bed While You Are Making Love?

	% YES	% NO	% YES, STAY ON BED
MEN	64	36	29
18–29	89	11	21
30–54	51	49	33
55+	66	34	32
WOMEN	67	33	37
18–29	93	7	50
30–54	56	44	40
55+	50	50	31

What Do We Do with Our Pets When We Make Love?

66 percent of pet owners do, indeed, let their pets stay in the room when they are making love. And it's overwhelmingly the youngest surveyed of each gender who are willing to put up with this additional audience. Of those who responded,

41 percent have dogs, 39 percent have cats, 11 percent have birds, and the rest have gerbils, snakes, fish, and other assorted critters.

More women (37 percent) than men (29 percent) allow their pets to stay on the bed while making love. Young women 18 to 29 are by far the nicest when it comes to granting this privilege, while their male counterparts seem to be the most territorial. This must lead to a great many dogfights in the bedroom, and gives new meaning to the term "petting."

Men, if you *don't like* pets in the room, be wary of the following kind of woman, who just *adores* having her pet in the bedroom. She's apt to be a small, left-handed woman with short hair, and she's a mother.

Women, the men who *love* pets in the boudoir are tall, long-haired, and right-handed. They claim to be slightly overweight and have no children of their own.

If the Phone Rings During the Height of Sex, Which One of the Following Things Are You Most Likely to Do:

	LET IT RING %	ANSWER IT AND:		
		TALK AND INTERRUPT SEX %	HAVE SEX WHILE TALKING %	TELL CALLER YOU'LL CALL BACK %
MEN	60	13	12	15
18–29	43	6	30	21
30–54	69	10	4	17
55+	62	20	10	8
WOMEN	65	13	20	10
18–29	66	9	23	2
30–54	66	13	14	7
55+	44	17	20	19

Let's hail those male 18-to-29ers and females over 55 for their stamina and their ability to handle multiple tasks much better than the other age brackets surveyed.

Don't forget to note that women have more of a proclivity to answer the phone without interruptus, in which category they outstrip the men (20 to 15 percent).

And for those who earn less than $25,000 a year . . . a whopping 79 percent like to let it ring, let it ring, let it ring!!!

How Much Time Usually Elapses in an Average Lovemaking Session from Start to Finish?

	MINUTES
MEN	21
18–29	19
30–54	18
55+	25
WOMEN	28
18–29	32
30–54	26
55+	25

Skip the Foreplay, Get the Stopwatch!

According to our survey, it takes 25 minutes and 34 seconds to enjoy a complete lovemaking session from start to finish.

The males told us it takes 21 minutes and 35 seconds, while the females report 28 minutes and 23 seconds. What happens during the 6-minute-and-49-second difference is anybody's guess.

The swiftest males are the 30-to-54-year-olds, who clock in at 18 minutes 33 seconds. The fastest females are those over 55, who clock in at 25 minutes 33 seconds.

A question for our readers: who are the partners of women 18 to 29, who report nearly 33 minutes of bliss? Whoever their partners are, they are certainly modest!

Now, get your stopwatch and your binoculars ready, to see if you agree with these profiles of the fastest and slowest men and women lovemakers:

FASTEST		SLOWEST	
MEN	**WOMEN**	**MEN**	**WOMEN**
Under $25,000	$25,000+	$25,000+	Under $25,000
High School	High School	College	College
Left-handed	Right-handed	Right-handed	Left-handed
Long hair	Short hair	Short Hair	Long Hair
Slim	Overweight	Overweight	Slim
Short	Tall	Tall	Short

Do You Like the Sheets to Be Tucked in Tightly at the Corners or to Hang Loosely Over the Sides of the Bed?

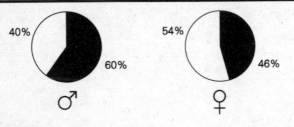

40%
60%
♂

54%
46%
♀

☐ TUCKED IN
TIGHTLY

■ HANGING
LOOSELY

When it comes to sheet-tucking or hanging, 54 percent of women like the sheets to be tucked in, while 60 percent of men prefer them to hang loosely.

The men adamant about having their sheets hang over the side of the bed earn less than $25,000, and are high-school-educated. The women who vote for neatly tucked in are likely to be tall and short-haired. They also happen to be left-handed.

Do You Read While in the Bathroom?

26%   20%   33%

74%   80%   67%

TOTAL   ♂   ♀

☐ YES
■ NO

Hand Me the Sports Section, Please!

Americans are a very literate breed . . . especially when it comes to bathroom reading. Nearly three-quarters (74 percent) of Americans confess to reading in the bathroom.

More men than women are bathroom readers—explaining why you see so many male coworkers walking away from their desks with a newspaper under their arms. And it's the high-school-educated bunch who are 12 percent more apt to grab a piece of the paper than their college counterparts.

On the Average, How Often Do You Initiate the Lovemaking Session?

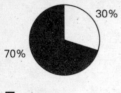

30%

70%

■ MEN
☐ WOMEN

Quite simply, aggressiveness in lovemaking starts with American men, who seem to be the initiators *70 percent* of the time.

The survey does uncover some female instigators out there. 7 percent of the women surveyed say they initiate lovemaking 100 percent of the time, with the majority of those women belonging in the 30-to-54 group. They might welcome an introduction to the 13 percent of men who also must always begin the lovemaking in their household.

And now we present the clues to the assertive women, or those who initiate lovemaking 70 to 90 percent of the time. She's a high-school-educated woman who earns under $25,000. Right-handed, she has short hair, claims to be a bit overweight, is small in stature, and has lots of kids.

Those men who initiate sex *less* than 20 percent of the time seem to be under-$25,000-earners with a college education, and are left-handed with long hair. Tall and skinny, they don't have any children. (*That* doesn't surprise us!)

Would You Like Your Mate to Be More or Less Aggressive During Lovemaking?

	% MORE	% LESS
MEN	**91**	**9**
18–29	91	9
30–54	98	2
55+	86	14
WOMEN	**68**	**32**
18–29	69	31
30–54	88	12
55+	43	57

All but 9 percent of the men surveyed opted for more aggressive behavior from their mates. It seems clear that they want the women to choose the position, the place, and the procedure!

A third of the females asked for the volume to be toned down, with women in the over-55 group voting loud and clear for a cessation of aggression.

Those women who want more forceful lovers tend to be short and slim, and have no kids. The men who desire more aggressive women are tall, a bit overweight, and also don't have any children.

And our results show that left-handed people are more aggressive than the right-handed when it comes to lovemaking.

How Many Intercourse Positions Do You Know?

# OF POSITIONS	1-3	4-6	7-9	10	11+	AVE. # KNOWN
% TOTAL SURVEYED	11	40	8	20	21	11.43
% MEN	7	49	4	13	27	13.55
18-29	8	33	1	23	34	17.58
30-54	12	48	6	17	17	8.41
55+	4	57	4	4	31	15.04
% WOMEN	14	32	12	28	14	9.10
18-29	20	40	15	15	10	9.55
30-54	11	27	11	38	12	8.00
55+	9	25	8	32	26	10.00

Where do *you* fit in? Men report they know 13.55 sexual positions, while women admit to knowing only 9.10 positions. So . . . who are the men showing those extra 4.45 positions to?

We're especially concerned about those women aged 30 to 54 who know the least variations of all—8.0. Perhaps the youngest group of men—who, with a whopping claim of 17.58 positions, *must* be the most innovative—should publish a training manual?

We took a very special look at the "know-it-alls"—that is, the group that says they know from 11 all the way up to 50 positions—and found a startling similarity: the men and women in this category are exactly alike. These people could be you or your best friends. So that you can identify them, here's what they look like: right-handed, and short in stature, they are college-educated. With long hair, yet little overall body hair, they claim to be a bit overweight and have lots of kids.

How Many Intercourse Positions Do You Regularly Use?

# OF POSITIONS	1–3	4–6	7–9	10	11 +	AVE. # USED
% TOTAL SURVEYED	55	34	2	5	4	4.49
% MEN	59	28	1	5	7	5.12
18–29	32	42	1	8	17	6.33
30–54	65	25	0	5	5	6.33
55 +	67	25	1	4	3	5.54
% WOMEN	48	41	4	5	2	3.82
18–29	44	39	9	4	4	4.17
30–54	53	42	0	5	0	3.63
55 +	53	40	0	7	0	3.53

Stop Wasting Those Positions!

Americans tend to use *less than half* of the number of positions they claim to know. And while men regularly use 5.12 positions, women only use 3.82. This means that the men are being selfish by keeping 1.30 positions to themselves! (Or that the women are just being lazy!)

The leading users of multiple positions are the men aged 18 to 29, who lay claim to more than 11. (We should hope so, since they claim to *know* nearly 18 of them!)

Do You Prefer to Shower/Bathe in the Morning, in the Evening, or Doesn't It Matter?

	% MORNING	% EVENING	% DOESN'T MATTER
% TOTAL SURVEYED	60	20	20
MEN	57	24	19
WOMEN	63	15	22

Morning bathing is the choice of 60 percent of Americans, while 20 percent prefer the evening. The remaining 20 percent don't really care one way or the other. But 83 percent and 71 percent of the men and women aged 18 to 29 vociferously cry for a morning rinse. Do they know something that we don't?

Do You Ever Invent a "Headache" or Other Excuse to Avoid Having to Make Love?

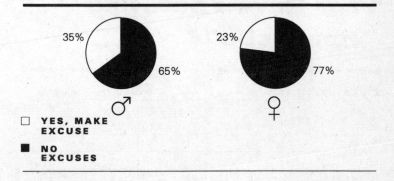

35%   65%   23%   77%

♂   ♀

☐ YES, MAKE EXCUSE

■ NO EXCUSES

Not Tonight, Honey, I Have a Headache!

Surprise, surprise; more men (35 percent) plead headache than do women (23 percent), with men in the 18-to-29-year-old group (43 percent) being the most likely to cop out. Another shibboleth knocked down.

Here are a few more tidbits to keep you on the lookout for these complainers. If the man sports long hair and is a bit overweight, he is a more likely candidate for the "not tonight, honey" syndrome. If the woman has short hair, is kind of underweight, and left-handed, you may be feeling a passion attack but she's probably developing a full-blown migraine.

Among Those Who Have Invented Headaches or Other Excuses: How Many Times in *the Past Year* Have You Cried "Headache"?

# OF TIMES	1	2	3	4	5-9	10 +	AVE. #
% MEN	8	14	29	3	23	23	6.3
18-29	9	8	26	7	22	27	6.7
30-54	7	8	30	6	26	23	6.1
55+	12	19	27	2	19	21	5.6
% WOMEN	10	10	10	26	33	11	5.2
18-29	6	12	14	20	31	17	4.8
30-54	12	8	8	21	37	14	5.6
55+	12	10	8	36	31	3	4.3

Cold Shower Anyone?

Younger men (18 to 29) and middle-aged women (30 to 54) develop the greatest number of headaches as passports away from sex.

The least headache-prone are those over 55. Both men and women in this age bracket rarely let pain get in nature's way.

The chronic (10+) men fakers are most likely to be those who earn over $25,000, have a college education, and no children. It's the tall, college-educated mothers who tend to be the ones most in need of the aspirin.

What Is Your Favorite Day of the Week for Sex?

	ANY	SUN	MON	TUE	WED	THUR	FRI	SAT
% TOTAL SURVEYED	64	18	1	1	1	1	6	8
% MEN	71	20	*	2	1	1	2	2
% WOMEN	58	15	3	0	1	1	10	12

* less than 1%

Always on Sunday?

64 percent of us don't have a favorite day of the week for sex. Apparently it doesn't matter *which* day it is; any day will do just fine, thank you!

That expression "Never on Sunday" certainly doesn't apply to sex. It turns out to be the favorite day of the week by a wide margin and boasts more than twice the score for Saturday, Americans' second favorite day, and three times that of Friday.

Speaking of Friday . . . men should be aware that it was the 10 percent women's vote that put Friday in third place. Thank goodness for Friday's triumph, for otherwise weekdays would be practically irrelevant when it comes to making love!

Women shouldn't even bother to consider Monday, because less than 1 percent of the men are available. Is "Monday Night Football" to blame? No wonder women veto Tuesday; they're still irritated about their partners' lack of response from the previous night!

Please Tell Us in Percentages How Often You Have Sex During the Following Times:

	A.M. WEEKENDS BEFORE BREAKFAST	P.M. 8–12	P.M. 5–8	A.M. BEFORE WORK	MIDNIGHT TO 6 A.M.	OTHER
% TOTAL SURVEYED	22	44	7	4	16	7
% MEN	23	48	6	4	12	7
% WOMEN	20	40	7	5	21	7

Overwhelmingly, the number-one time slot for making love is between 8:00 P.M. and midnight. Second on the list is before breakfast on weekends. What a nice way to start your day: sex first and Wheaties afterward.

The most interesting statistic is the third most favorite time, which is between midnight and 6:00 A.M. Twice as many women (21 percent) as men prefer this time, so women, set your alarms, wake your man, and show him this page! By the way, these "night owls" tend to be from the 18-to-29 set, are high-school-educated, and earn less than $25,000. They probably derive their extra "get-up-and-go" from the fact that they usually don't have any children.

The "early-morning-weekend-before-breakfast" lovers tend to be older couples—perhaps "empty nesters"—who earn over $25,000 and are high-school-educated. They give new meaning to the expression "breakfast in bed."

How Long Do You Think You Could Live Comfortably Without Sex?

	A DAY	A WEEK	MONTH/ FEW MONTHS	A YEAR	FOREVER
% MEN	17	31	46	3	3
18–29	27	17	42	8	6
30–54	12	30	43	5	10
55 +	10	37	48	-	5
% WOMEN	13	10	61	12	4
18–29	14	8	50	13	15
30–54	5	10	73	10	2
55 +	7	13	60	13	7

Overall, 53 percent of our respondents can do without sex for "a month to a few months." After that? Well, 20 percent of us (31 percent of men and 10 percent of women) could last for a week.

And let's hear it for those willpower champions: the 17 percent of men and 13 percent of women who said they could wait *one whole day* without sex. Pretty scary, if you think about how many of us take extended business trips . . . or two-week vacations.

What we want to know is who are the 4 percent who tell us that they could wait *forever*? We think it's time for these respondents to find new partners—and quickly!

Back to the willpower champions. The women earn under $25,000, are college-educated, and are mothers. They are right-handed and short in stature. The men also earn less than $25,000, but they are high-school-educated and left-handed. They claim to be a bit overweight and—no surprise about it—are fathers.

Have You Ever Showered with Your Partner?

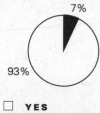

7%

93%

☐ YES
■ NO

Everyone into the Shower!

Showering with your mate appears to be a great national pastime; nearly all of us do it at one time or another!

So let's focus on the nonconformists: the 7 percent who do not shower with their mates at all. More often than not these people are parents. Probably they have *lots* of children who go a long way toward preventing them from enjoying the intimacy of a mutual shower.

The majority from this group of solitary showerers are college-educated and earn over $25,000 a year. The women have short hair, while the men are likely to be slightly overweight left-handers.

Do You Generally Keep Your Eyes Open or Shut When You Kiss?

	% OPEN	% SHUT
% TOTAL SURVEYED	20	80
% MEN	27	73
18–29	34	66
30–54	15	85
55+	30	70
% WOMEN	13	87
18–29	13	87
30–54	16	84
55+	9	91

Do We Kiss Like They Do in the Movies?

This is an open-and-shut case! Shut-eyes definitely have it! Yet twice as many men (27 percent) kiss with their eyes wide open as women (13 percent).

Both the young men (18 to 29) and the older men (55+) are the most likely open-eyed kissers. But older women won't be caught dead taking a peek (only 9 percent kiss with their eyes open).

The eye-opening male kisser has a definite profile. He has long hair and is left-handed. He's also a bit overweight, is shorter than average, and has no children.

The female eye-openers are harder to profile; all we know is that they are tall and right-handed, and that they are mothers.

Do You Usually Make Love with the Lights On?

	% ON	% OFF
% TOTAL SURVEYED	38	62

Lights, Action, Camera!!!

As you can see, 38 percent of Americans prefer making love with the lights on, while the majority (62 percent) prefer smooching in the dark!

Those who enjoy the light are most likely to be couples who do not have children (perhaps *that's* the reason they can leave the lights on) or those who earn the big bucks ($25,000+) and obviously can afford the extra electricity.

A few more interesting facts that came to light: 72 percent of those with high-school educations prefer the dark. Left-handed women prefer lights *off*, while right-handed women prefer lights *on*. Yet the majority of left-handed men prefer lights *on*, and vice versa for the right-handed guys. Talk about crossover!

Is there anyone out there who can figure any of this out? We're in the dark!

What Do You Generally Like to Do After Sex?

	% MEN	% WOMEN
Sleep	69	47
Cuddle	32	54
Bathroom	28	42
Talk	20	42
TV	15	20
Smoke	16	14
Eat	15	14
Read	4	4
Go home	2	2

(NOTE: Totals add up to more than 100 percent due to multiple answers.)

22 percent more men than women prefer to doze after sex . . . while 22 percent more women than men want to cuddle. And it's the women who prefer to talk more after a rendezvous! In most other respects, however, men and women answered in sync.

Our favorite response to this question comes from the 2 percent of each gender who simply replied, "After making love I generally go home!"

Do You and Your Mate Use the Bathroom at the Same Time?

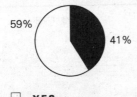

59% 41%

☐ YES
■ NO

This may surprise some people, and then again, maybe it won't; 59 percent of Americans use the bathroom at the same time as their mates. And it is the oldest respondents (55+) who are the *least* likely to have a simultaneous sharing of La Toilette.

The 18-to-29-year-old group for both genders seems to have that "together" feeling even when it comes to matters of the toilette. Nearly 80 percent told us that it is "no big deal" and happens all the time. This attitude *must* be tied to the fact that this same age group is also the most likely to shower with their partners.

Do You Ever Wear Sexy Underwear?

Among Those Who Do, Did You Buy Them Yourself or Did Someone Else Buy Them?

	% YES	% NO	% I BOUGHT THEM
MEN	**54**	**46**	**50**
18–29	72	28	39
30–54	46	54	36
55+	51	49	69
WOMEN	**84**	**16**	**86**
18–29	96	4	81
30–54	78	22	86
55+	80	20	90

More than two-thirds (68 percent) of Americans admit to wearing "sexy" underwear, with 30 percent more women willing to don silky undergarments than men.

The sexiest underwear wearers are those aged 18 to 29, where an overwhelming 96 percent of the women wear beautiful lingerie and 72 percent of the men do likewise. Even those over 55 are actively involved in the sexy-underwear revolution, with 80 percent of the women and 51 percent of the men participating. What's going on with those in their middle years? Both sexes in the 30-to-54 age range are the least likely to wear tantalizing tidbits.

70 percent of us buy our *own* intimate apparel, thank you. But while an overwhelming number of women (86 percent) buy their own undies, 50 percent of men leave their sexiness in underwear to their women.

Do You Usually Undress in Front of Your Mate?

12%

88%

☐ YES
■ NO

An overwhelming 88 percent of Americans undress regularly in front of their mates, with men 10 percent more likely to bare it all than women.

The only major oddity found in the results was the modesty exhibited among the women in the 55+ age group, where 36 percent of the women do not undress in front of their mates. All of the other age groups showed both men and women to be virtually alike in this habit.

Have You Ever Worn Your Partner's Underwear?

	% YES	% NO
MEN	**19**	**81**
18–29	39	61
30–54	12	88
55+	13	87
WOMEN	**25**	**75**
18–29	32	68
30–54	18	82
55+	24	76

Anyone Seen My Underwear?

More women (25 percent) say that they sometimes wear their mates' underwear, with 19 percent of men confessing to wearing their ladies' undies. But, obviously, this isn't a favorite national pastime.

The best bet for finding a man who wears women's underwear is to look for a tall, right-handed, and long-haired guy who is 18-to-29 years old and earns over $25,000 a year. The woman most likely to be wearing her man's briefs is in the same age group, height range, and income bracket as the previous. However, she is likely to have short hair.

Have You Ever Exaggerated Your Attributes by Stuffing Something in Your Shorts or Your Bra?

	% HAVE STUFFED	% HAVEN'T STUFFED
MEN	4	96
WOMEN	8	92

To Show the Truth or Not to Show the Truth . . . That Is the Question

Stuffing does not seem to be the rage—or, at least, hardly anyone *admits* to it. 94 percent deny *ever* having done such a dastardly deed . . . although we wonder how many might have contemplated it but simply feared getting caught?!

It should be duly noted that twice as many women as men are stuffers, although neither number is truly significant. Women 30-to-54 are the most likely stuffers (12 percent), with the 55+ group a close second (9 percent).

In the strange-but-true category, we find that both the women and men stuffers share two things in common: they tend to be left-handed and have no children. Any ideas why?

Do You Wash Your Hair First, Last, or in the Middle of a Shower?

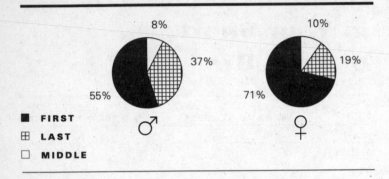

8% 37% 55% ♂

10% 19% 71% ♀

■ FIRST
⊞ LAST
☐ MIDDLE

63 percent of us will wash our hair first when we get into the shower. The rest of us (28 percent) will do it at the end of a shower, and 9 percent will do it in the middle. Thanks to science and Johnson's Baby Shampoo, you can get suds in your eyes at any time.

An especially interesting tidbit: left-handed men do it last (63 percent), while left-handed women do it first (65 percent).

Do You Prefer to Be on the Top or Bottom During Intercourse?

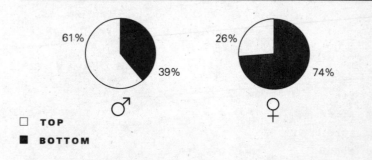

61%   39%   26%   74%

♂   ♀

☐ TOP
■ BOTTOM

It's a Topsy-Turvy World!

The majority of Americans seem to be sticking to the good old-fashioned way, with 61 percent of men preferring the top and 74 percent of women preferring the bottom.

There is, however, a chance that a new pattern is emerging: 39 percent of men are asking for the bottom and 26 percent of women are opting for the top. The most pronounced age categories for this trend are men 18 to 29, 48 percent of whom prefer the bottom, and women 55 and over, 39 percent of whom prefer the top.

Would You Have Sex with an Attractive Stranger for Money?

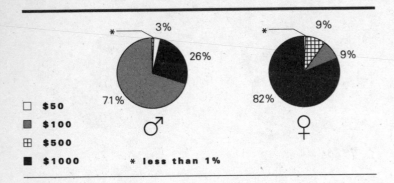

3%

*

26%

9%

*

9%

71%

♂

82%

♀

- ☐ **$50**
- ▨ **$100**
- ⊞ **$500**
- ■ **$1000**   * less than 1%

What's the Value of a Dollar?

Only a handful of mercenary males would have sex with an attractive female stranger if they were paid $50 . . . yet 71 percent of the men say they can be bought for $100.

Women, on the other hand, proved to be more selective. Only a few would take $100 or $500 and *none* would take $50. The magic price for them seems to be $1,000. It seems that women place a higher value on intimacy than men! And although we didn't offer the option of "no money at all," we're now beginning to wonder how many—especially from the women—would have opted for this category. (We're not really wondering about it for the men!)

In the category of "strange but true," why is it that we found that people who earn less than $25,000 a year were willing to wait for the ante to be increased, while those who earn substantially more dollars were more inclined to take the first offer?

Have You Ever Had Sex with More than One Person in a 24-Hour Period?

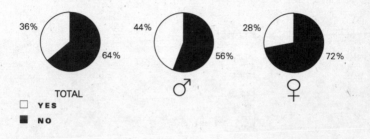

36%   44%   28%

64%   56%   72%

TOTAL   ♂   ♀

□ YES
■ NO

Our results show that the most promiscuous group is the 30-to-54 segment for both sexes. Both men and women in this bracket far surpassed the norms for their respective sexes, with 50 and 36 percent, respectively.

Okay, get ready for the tidbits on those who told us that they have slept with more than one person in a 24-hour period. The women and men in this segment are strikingly alike, with the only point of difference being that the women are right-handed and the men are left-handed. These extremely "sex-driven" folks are likely to be college-educated, and earn over $25,000. They are long-haired, a bit overweight, short in stature (but not in sex drive), and while they have lots of body hair, they don't have any kids.

What One Part of Your Body Do You Consider Your Best?

Listed in order of popularity

MEN	WOMEN
Butt	Breasts
Legs	Face
Face	Legs
Arms	Butt
Head	Eyes
Tongue (?!)	Thighs
Penis	Waist
Chest	Vagina
Brain	Nose
Eyes	Calves

What One Part of Your Body Do You Consider Your Worst?

Listed starting with the least favorite

MEN	WOMEN
Stomach	Stomach
Feet	Butt
Chest	Hips
Knees	Legs
Legs	Thighs
Butt	Breasts
Nose	Eyes
Tongue (?!)	Feet
Penis	Lips

Do You Refer to Your Mate by Any Special or Pet Name?

MEN

Babe
Honey
Gumby
Bean
Lady
Banker
Fuzzy
Snuggle bunny
Big Kahuna
Sweetheart
Sugarplum
Mouth
Motor mouth
Lovey

WOMEN

Honeybunch
Dear
Honey
Cuddles
Bunkie
Dreamboat
Moron
George
Boogie
Sweet pea
Muttonchop
Brisket face
Stupid
Romeo
Tarzan
Stud
Studley

Do You Pee
in the Shower?

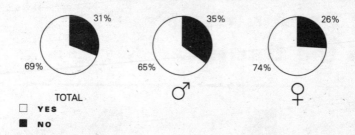

31%

69%

35%

65%

26%

74%

TOTAL

♂

♀

☐ YES

■ NO

Americans do, in fact, pee while in the shower, and women are even more likely to do it than men. 74 percent of the women and 65 percent of the men combine the functions of their water closet and shower.

The women and men who do tend to be $25,000+ earners, college-educated, and right-handers. The women are tall and long-haired, while the men are short and heavier than the norm.

And while women 30-to-54 are most likely to pee in the shower (81 percent), men in the same age group are *least* likely, with a low of 45 percent. Go figure!

What Side of the Bed Do You Sleep On (From the Perspective of Facing the Head of the Bed)?

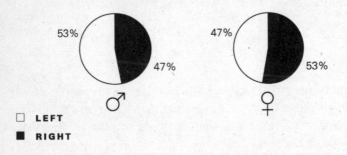

53% 47%

47% 53%

♂ ♀

☐ LEFT
■ RIGHT

Women on the right and men on the left are the preferred sleeping positions . . . but not by much.

Why do you suppose that the only age group that sleeps differently is the 55+ group, where men prefer the right and women the left?

It is interesting to note that 63 percent of left-handed men and 57 percent of left-handed women sleep on the right side of the bed. When it comes to right-handers, 45 percent of the men sleep on the left and 54 percent of the women sleep on the left.

Do You Sleep in the Nude, in Pajamas, in Underwear, or Something Else?

	IN THE NUDE	PAJAMAS	UNDERWEAR	SOMETHING ELSE
% MEN	53	10	33	4
% WOMEN	27	34	12	27

For men, nudity is in and PJs are out; Sears and JCPenney, be forewarned! While overall 40 percent of us are likely to sleep in the nude, 53 percent of men sleep in the buff! But that's not all: the "nudest" snoozers are these 18-to-29-year-old men and women (58 and 32 percent, respectively).

Most women prefer to wear PJs, but what we're intrigued by is the "something else" that 27 percent of women claim to put on. Would it be some type of silky teddy—or something else, like her man's top shirt?!

Those women who sleep in the nude are likely to be tall and slender and have no children who could creep in on them. Like the women, the bare-it-all men are without kids, but they claim to be a bit overweight and are short in stature.

If You Have Children, Do You Always Wait to Have Sex Until They Are Sleeping?

	% YES	% NO
% TOTAL SURVEYED	41	59
MEN	40	60
18–29	50	50
30–54	62	38
55+	26	74
WOMEN	44	56
18–29	86	14
30–54	33	67
55+	31	69

On the average, unity won out over discretion, 59 to 41 percent. But the younger the woman, the less likely she is to indulge in lovemaking while the patter of little feet might venture into the bedroom. The older the woman, the more she throws caution to the winds. And for men 55 and over . . . well, you see our results. No comment!

The in-a-hurry, can't-wait-for-the-kids-to-fall-asleep crowd seems to fit a very definite profile. Both the men and women are college-educated, left-handed, and long-haired. They both report that they are tall and slender, with lots of body hair.

Have You Ever Made Love in One of Your Children's Beds?

23%

77%

☐ YES
■ NO

Americans can be naughty and bawdy and all that stuff. 23 percent of Americans reported that their tot's bed was just right when it came to finding a launching pad for their amorous inclinations. But the majority refrain from just such an activity.

It's mostly tall men who are $25,000+ earners, high-school-educated, right-handed, and long-haired who have experienced love in a child's bed. In contrast, the women generally sport short hair, are short in stature, and left-handed. They earn under $25,000 a year, have a high-school education, and are thin.

Do You Wash Your Hands in a Public Bathroom After Using the Facilities?

Do You Wash Your Hands If You Are Alone in the Public Bathroom?

	% YES	% NO	% EVEN WHEN ALONE
MEN	89	11	78
WOMEN	95	5	89

Nearly all of us wash our hands in a public toilet after using the facilities, with those over 55 being the most fastidious (men: 97 percent; women: 99 percent).

But when no one else is around, 11 percent fewer men and 6 percent fewer women take the time to wash up. We only hope that these figures are not representative of the restaurant employees who completed this survey!

Do Men Wash One Hand or Both Hands After Using the Urinal?

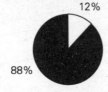

12%

88%

☐ ONE
■ BOTH

All Hands Down!

An overwhelming 88 percent of men don't cheat by washing only one hand after bathroom duty. But beware of those who earn over $25,000 a year, are college-educated, and left-handed. These men constitute the likely 12 percent who wash only one hand after using the urinal in a public facility. Maybe they're practicing water conservation, or perhaps they feel it's just a case of pure and simple logic?!

Do You Indulge in Oral Sex?

15%
85%

13%
87%

18%
82%

♂

♀

TOTAL
☐ YES
■ NO

In 1940 this question never would have been thought of, let alone asked. In 1970 it *would* have been thought of but not asked. But today . . . anything goes! And 87 percent of men and 82 percent of women indulge in oral sex.

The response was highly favorable across all age groups, including 80 percent of men and 73 percent of women in the over-55 group.

More college-educated respondents (91 percent) indulge than participants from the other demographic groupings. Do you suppose it's one of those liberal-arts electives?

This Is a Five-Part Question About Oral Sex for Those Who Indulge.

Do You Prefer Doing It Simultaneously with Your Partner or One Person at a Time? Which Do You Like Better, Giving or Receiving Oral Sex? Or Both?

	SIMUL-TANEOUSLY	ONE AT A TIME	GIVING	RECEIV-ING	BOTH
% MEN	32	68	9	35	56
% WOMEN	44	56	11	37	52

The Final Word on Oral Sex!

Men prefer it one at a time (68 percent) as do a majority of the women (56 percent).

Only 10 percent of the sexes prefer being on the *giving* end of oral sex, compared with the 36 percent who enjoy being on the *receiving* end. In fact, less than 1 percent of men over 55, and only 5 percent of women 18-to-29, claim that they want to give. The remaining 54 percent delight in giving and receiving alike. So, is it or isn't it better to give than to receive?

The men who prefer it one at a time are a virtual perfect match for the women who tell us they prefer it simultaneously. The following are the features they have in common: right-handed, short-haired, thin, short in stature, a lot of body hair, and no kids.

Have You Ever Slept with Someone on the First Date?

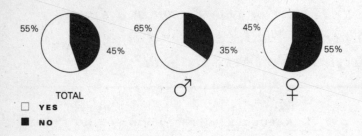

55% 45% 65% 35% 45% 55%

TOTAL ♂ ♀

☐ YES
■ NO

More than one half (55 percent) of all Americans have revealed that they slept with someone on the first date, with 20 percent more men claiming to have taken this plunge.

The profile of these impulsive people shows both sexes to be quite similar. They both have long hair, are left-handed, and they don't have any kids. They differ in that the men are tall but slightly overweight, while the women are short but thin.

Have You Ever Slept with Someone and Then Forgotten Their Name?

36% 64% ♂

25% 75% ♀

☐ YES
■ NO

I Never Will Forget What's Her (or His) Name

36 percent of men and 25 percent of women told us that they can't recall the name of someone they've slept with. The most forgetful group is the 30-to-54-year-olds, where both the men and women are tops in forgetfulness.

Isn't it reassuring to know that a full two-thirds of the Americans surveyed are ready, willing, and able to recall their partners' names? Fantastic!

This question yielded another set of those startling but true findings that tell us that the forgetful group is virtually the same for both men and women. College-educated and earning over $25,000, they tend to be left-handed and have long hair. Both are tall and weigh more than the norm. Is this the profile of anyone you know or love?

Have You Ever Had Sex with More Than One Person at the Same Time?

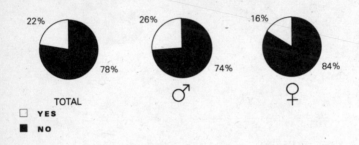

22%   26%   16%

78%   74%   84%

TOTAL   ♂   ♀

☐ YES
■ NO

Is There Someone Else Here with Us?

Most of the time—no. Only 22 percent of Americans reported having sex with more than one person at a time. However, the men reported engaging in this activity significantly more often than did the women.

Seems to us that the colleges and universities must be offering some new experiences that older folks never even dreamed of, thought of, or cared for. College-educated people are twice as likely to have participated in group sex as their high-school-educated counterparts.

One other oddity exists. It seems that short men and tall women are much more likely to have engaged in group sex than their counterparts.

Do You Always Flush the Toilet in a Public Facility?

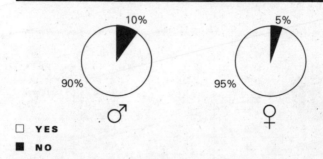

10%

5%

90%

95%

♂

♀

☐ YES

■ NO

We always thought Americans were fairly sanitary and our belief has been bolstered by the results of this survey, which shows that an overwhelming *93 percent* of us will take the time to make sure that the job is totally finis.

There are, however, a few people we should watch. Keep your eyes open for the 5 percent of women who fail to flush. Pass the word and remind them to do what they would want the person before them to do. 10 percent of men likewise need to be reminded of this common courtesy. Luckily all of these offenders are easy to spot. They are 30-to-54 years old and earn less than $25,000. The men are short, and the women are tall, and they all probably sport furtive looks on their faces.

When You Make Love, Which of the Following Best Describes What Occurs?

	WE ARE BOTH SILENT	BOTH TALK	I AM SILENT MATE TALKS	I TALK MATE SILENT
% MEN	**32**	**48**	**9**	**11**
18–29	17	67	11	5
30–54	29	51	8	12
55+	42	37	7	14
% WOMEN	**24**	**53**	**12**	**11**
18–29	18	55	9	18
30–54	30	47	20	3
55+	24	52	12	12

Is It Shhh! When Making Love, or Is It Yak, Yak, Yak?

Wonder why it is that both younger men and women claim that they converse with their partners in bed (67 and 55 percent, respectively), while the older set claims to hardly *ever* utter a word (7 and 12 percent, respectively)?

The younger talkers are easily identified in our survey, what with both sexes being right-handed and long-haired. The men, however, tended to be slightly overweight, while the women were fairly slender.

The older set who were loath to utter a word are slightly overweight, with shorter hair for both, and very much in love!

Have You Ever Made Love with Someone:
10 Years Younger
10 Years Older
20 Years Younger
20 Years Older?

	10 YRS. YOUNGER	10 YRS. OLDER	20 YRS. YOUNGER	20 YRS. OLDER
% MEN	**49**	**49**	**21**	**33**
18–29	14	43	14	43
30–54	50	75	17	50
55+	60	35	25	20
% WOMEN	**19**	**90**	**3**	**32**
18–29	9	90	1	18
30–54	25	91	1	42
55+	25	88	13	38

(NOTE: Above percentages add to more than 100 due to multiple answers.)

For this question, men and women really proved to have separate preferences. Let's talk about the men first. 49 percent of men have made love to women 10 years younger than themselves, while an equal number have made love to women 10 years older. 21 percent of men have reached back 20 years, while 33 percent have reached ahead 20 years.

On the distaff side, women clearly go for older men as *90 percent* have made love to men 10 years older, and 32 percent have made love to men 20 years older. Only 19 percent of women have made love to a man 10 years their junior. Seems that the majority of women still prefer older men!

We are particularly intrigued by the possibilities of men 18-to-29 years old making love to women 20 years younger. Whatever happened to just playing with Barbie dolls and G.I. Joes? Or is it just that some of our respondents went a little overboard in trying to impress?

Here is a profile of the more likely lovers by sex and age:

MADE LOVE TO SOMEONE 10 YEARS YOUNGER
MEN: Under $25,000, high-school education, right-handed
WOMEN: Under $25,000, college education, left-handed

MADE LOVE TO SOMEONE 10 YEARS OLDER
MEN: $25,000+, high-school education, long-haired
WOMEN: Under $25,000, college education, left-handed

MADE LOVE TO SOMEONE 20 YEARS YOUNGER
MEN: $25,000+, high-school education, thin, no kids
WOMEN: Under $25,000, college education, short, left-handed

MADE LOVE TO SOMEONE 20 YEARS OLDER
MEN: Under $25,000, college education, short-haired, tall
WOMEN: $25,000+, college education, short, left-handed

This question provoked quite a response from our respondents. "I am 81 years old, and I very much enjoy making love to my girlfriend, who is 37 years old. P.S. She says I am the best lover she has ever had.''

"I am a 52-year-old divorcée who finds herself very much attracted to young men—the younger the better. Recently I made love to a 17-year-old for five nonstop hours.''

"I am a 51-year-old male who has been madly in love with a woman who is now 72 years old. We have been together for the past 15 years and she is the best thing that has ever happened to me since my divorce from a woman only two years younger than me.''

"As a 22-year-old senior at a major university in the south, I have found that the male students just do not satisfy me sexually or intellectually. Therefore, I have been dating one of the professors, who is 53 years old. He is a wonderful lover and intellect and we have many things in common.''

Who Is More Romantic, You or Your Mate?

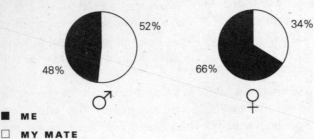

52%

48%

♂

34%

66%

♀

■ ME
□ MY MATE

Romance, romance . . . who is more romantic? Our results show that women have the edge, but basically that's because 80 percent of the women aged 30-to-54 ardently declared that they loved flowers, moonlight, and candles!

As you can see, the majority of men (52 percent) tell us that the ladies in their lives are more romantic. The women also tell us that they (66 percent) are the more romantic by far.

It's interesting to know that 58 percent of men aged 18-to-29 were willing to admit to a tender side . . . wonder if they've taken the current notion that women prefer sensitive men to heart?

Want to know who the most romantic people are? Well, our survey shows *him* to be right-handed, short-haired, and a bit overweight. Short in stature, he is a parent.

She mirrors quite the same characteristics as her partner in romance in terms of height and hair length. Where she differs from him is that she is left-handed, thin, and has no kids at all.

Do You Snore?

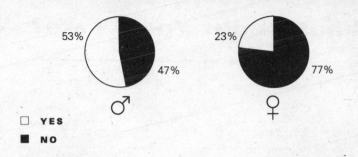

53%
47%

♂

23%
77%

♀

☐ YES
■ NO

Just as romance seems to belong to the women, snoring appears to be a province of the men. 53 percent of the men snore, while only 23 percent of the women do or at least admit to it!

Those *least* likely to snore? According to their mates, it's women in the 18-to-29-year-old age group.

Do You Talk in Your Sleep? What About Your Mate?

	% YES	% NO	YES, MATE TALKS IN SLEEP
% MEN	41	59	28
18–29	67	33	44
30–54	30	70	23
55+	38	62	18
% WOMEN	36	64	24
18–29	44	56	27
30–54	43	57	29
55+	13	87	14

More men than women talk in their sleep. But it's those young men who must have a great deal on their minds, as 67 percent of them are chatterers!

The most tight-lipped group of all is women 55 and over, who seem to keep it all to themselves.

More people *think* they talk in their sleep than is reported by their mates. 38 percent of the total surveyed told us that *they* talk in their sleep, but only 26 percent of their mates reported that to be the truth. Hopefully, this statistic will relieve a lot of people!

Do Men Shave and Then Shower, or Shower and Then Shave?

46% 54%

☐ SHAVE FIRST
■ SHOWER FIRST

Men are almost evenly divided when it comes to answering this question. The shower-first group at 54 percent is a bit ahead of the 46 percent who shave first.

The differences that we found within this question crossed the income and education barriers, where we found that those earning less than $25,000 and who have a high-school education are more likely to shave and then shower, while their counterparts do the opposite.

So the moral to all of this is that whatever you choose to do—shave, then shower; shower, then shave—you have a lot of support. You're not alone.

Are Men Satisfied with the Size of Their Penis?

35%

65%

☐ YES
■ NO

The medical and scientific community will be alarmed to know that only two-thirds (65 percent) of the men in the United States are satisfied with the size of their penis. They had better get started with some research to help these men out!

Geneticists, get your notebooks ready. The following is a list of the corrections that the men voted for. Among the dissatisfied, 52 percent wish for *bigness*, while 12 percent want it to be *smaller*. 53 percent said they would like theirs to be *longer*, and 40 percent want theirs to be *wider*.

Okay, now we'd like to know who the 12 percent are who want their penis to be smaller. How big *are* you guys, and does your partner have a problem with it? The guys who *claim* to want it smaller are likely to be 18 to 29, high-school-educated, and a little overweight. They earn less than $25,000 a year and are very tall.

And, oh, yes, they probably have a perpetual smile on their faces!

Are Women Satisfied with the Size of Their Mates' Penis?

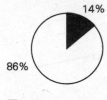

14%

86%

☐ YES
■ NO

Men, heave a deep sigh of relief: 86 percent of the women declare themselves to be satisfied. And give a round of applause for those 18-to-29-year-old women who earn less than $25,000 a year; they claim to be the happiest of them all (96 percent)!

Among those who are dissatisfied, 44 percent would like it to be *bigger*, and 22 percent would like it to be *smaller*. 48 percent of the women would like their mates to have *longer* penises and 23 percent are looking for them to have *wider* ones.

The long and the short of this question is that it takes all sorts to make the world go around.

Are Women Satisfied with the Size of Their Breasts?

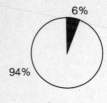

6%

94%

☐ YES

■ NO

Virtually all of the women in our survey have told us that they are satisfied with the size of their breasts (94 percent).

Of the 6 percent who are not satisfied, 5 percent would like to have larger breasts, while only 1 percent said that they would like to have them smaller.

In the final analysis, then, the women are more satisfied with what they have than are the men. Does this surprise anyone?

Are Men Satisfied with the Size of Their Mates' Breasts?

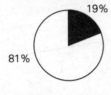

19%

81%

☐ YES
■ NO

Only 19 percent of men are not satisfied with the size of their mates' breasts. Yet when asked whether they would want the breasts to be bigger or smaller, virtually all said bigger (99 percent)!

Those who are unsatisfied earn over $25,000 a year, are college-educated, have long hair, and are quite greedy!

When we cross-tabulate these results regarding satisfaction with penis size, we find that the same men tend to be very content all around! Of the men who are satisfied with the size of their own penis, 89 percent are also satisfied with their mates' breast size!

Do You Listen to the Radio While Using the Bathroom?

	% YES	% NO
MEN	**36**	**64**
18–29	50	50
30–54	15	85
55+	43	57
WOMEN	**37**	**63**
18–29	48	52
30–54	32	68
55+	27	73

More than one-third of us (36 percent) like to listen to the radio while in the bathroom. The yuppies (18 to 29) of both genders like it to a much higher degree than any other group.

"Opposites attract" is a very common saying, and it holds true for this question. Our analysis shows that the men who like to listen to the radio in the bathroom have profiles that are exactly opposite from that of the women:

MEN: $25,000+, college-educated, left-handed

WOMEN: under $25,000, high-school-educated, right-handed

Have You Ever Done a Striptease for Your Mate?

	% YES	% NO
MEN	**45**	**55**
18–29	52	48
30–54	33	67
55+	51	49
WOMEN	**65**	**35**
18–29	61	39
30–54	50	50
55+	81	19

Take It Off, Take It All Off, Dear!

More than one-half (55 percent) of all Americans have done a striptease for their mates. 65 percent of women and 45 percent of men reported indulging in this form of entertainment for their loves.

This kind of performance shows no age barriers, because women over 55 (81 percent) are the most likely of all. And their male counterparts are not far behind either, with 51 percent engaging in this tantalizing activity.

At the other end of the age spectrum is the talented 18-to-29-year-old group, in which 52 percent of the men and 61 percent of the women report having peeled off the layers.

Has Anyone Ever Inadvertently Entered the Room When You Were Having Sex?

The Oops! Factor

35 percent of Americans have experienced the oops! factor while making love.

And for men 18-to-29, 72 percent of whom proudly proclaim they've never been caught: just wait until you have kids! The oops! factor is caused mostly by children (79 percent), followed by parents (27 percent), and siblings (6 percent).

Have You Ever Inadvertently Entered a Room Where Someone Was Having Sex?

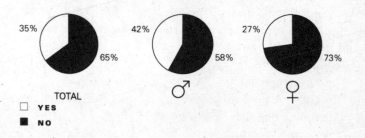

35% | 65%

42% | 58% ♂

27% | 73% ♀

TOTAL

☐ YES
■ NO

Sorry, I Was Looking for My Coat!

The prior question asked if anyone had ever entered a room in which lovemaking was going on. 35 percent replied in the affirmative. We turned the question around and found that an identical 35 percent in fact have had the shoe on the other foot—that is, inadvertently entering a room where someone else was having sex. Men (42 percent) are more likely to have surprised a couple in the act than women (27 percent).

We applaud women 55 and over, who were the females most likely to have someone enter the room while they were having a good time (36 percent), but who have learned from their experience and barely ever intrude themselves (20 percent)! Young men 18-to-29, 53 percent of whom interrupted but who have only been the interruptees 22 percent of the time—learn to be more aware! If you were interrupted more often, we're sure you'd learn more caution when the shoe is on—or off—the other foot.

Those who have entered the room, only to be the surpriser instead of the surprisee, have slipped out (79 percent), interrupted the act (18 percent), or halted it altogether (3 percent). The latter must have been the parents of the people who were otherwise occupied!

We wonder why the college-educated, $25,000+ group are 20 percent more likely to intrude than any other group. Could it be that they are:

(a) absentminded?
(b) rich enough to afford big houses with so many rooms that they get lost?
(c) peeping toms at heart?
(d) all of the above?
(e) none of the above?

Have You Ever Had Sex While Someone Else Was in the Room?

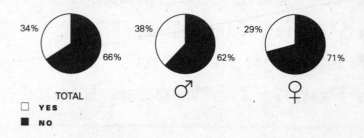

34%
66%

38%
62%
♂

29%
71%
♀

TOTAL

□ YES
■ NO

Three's Company—Four's Company—Five's Company. Six May Be a Crowd

We had a few people who actually asked us, "Isn't there *always* someone else in the room when you have sex?" Cut it out, wise guys. Anyhow, 34 percent of the respondents to the survey indicated that indeed they have had sex while someone else was in the room.

The 18-to-29 generation for both genders is the most likely by far (40 percent for women, 44 percent for men) to engage in this rather unusual behavior. Obviously, they have fewer inhibitions! (And wouldn't you like to be one of them?)

Most of those who indulge in this activity tend to be tall, right-handed, and childless. The men sport short hair, while the women have long hair.

Have You Ever Written Someone's Number on a Public Bathroom Wall?

Have You Ever *Called* a Phone Number That You Copied from a Public Bathroom Wall?

	% YES	% NO	ACTUALLY CALLED NUMBER
% MEN	**18**	**82**	**13**
18–29	25	75	8
30–54	15	85	5
55+	17	83	20
% WOMEN	**10**	**90**	**2**
18–29	4	96	1
30–54	14	86	5
55+	13	87	1

An overwhelming majority of Americans (86 percent) have never written a number down? Where then, do all those numbers come from?

Everywhere you go you find numbers, numbers, numbers on the walls. Our analysis of the writers and the callers indicates that they are one and the same. That is to say, the profile of the people who say they *write* someone's name on the wall is exactly the same as those who actually *called* a number written on the wall.

Since you're dying to find out who these sexual pen pals are: they are under-$25,000 earners, high-school-educated, right-handed, tall, and slim. They also don't have any kids. And keep an eye out for younger men, since one out of four owns up to this dastardly deed.

Do You Neatly Fold or Crumple Your Toilet Tissue?

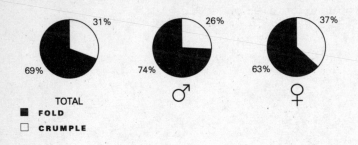

31%

26%

37%

69%

74%

63%

TOTAL

♂

♀

■ FOLD
□ CRUMPLE

The toilet-tissue folders are free to rejoice over the results, which tell us that folders (69 percent) have it over the crumplers (31 percent) by a wide margin! Every age group, income group, and educational group that we polled leaned heavily in favor of folding.

More right-handed men are folders than left-handers: the reverse is true of the women. (No, we can't figure this statistic out either!)

Let's flush this age-old battle between the fussy folders and the rumpled crumplers down the toilet forever . . . along with the "over or under" spool debate (where *over* the spool is preferred by a wide margin, 68 to 32 percent).

Which of the Following Best Describes Any Birth Control Methods That You and Your Partner Use:

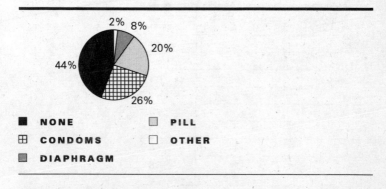

2% 8%

20%

44%

26%

■ NONE ▨ PILL

⊞ CONDOMS ☐ OTHER

▨ DIAPHRAGM

What Types of Birth Control Are Used These Days?

While some people reported using more than one method, over 44 percent of our respondents don't use anything at all! Some of them are over 55, some wish to be parents, and some don't use anything for religious reasons. We will, of course, excuse these people for skewing these statistics. But for those who just can't be bothered, you had best be hoping for some wee little ones, because you'll find that the pitter-patter of tiny feet around the house no longer belongs to just the family pet!

Would You Be Embarrassed to Buy Condoms from a Salesperson of the Opposite Sex?

	% YES	% NO
MEN	23	77
18–29	38	62
30–54	16	84
55+	19	81
WOMEN	26	74
18–29	27	73
30–54	44	56
55+	12	88

Excuse Me, Could I Please Have Some, Er, Er, Er. . . a Package of Gum, a Copy of Time Magazine, and Er, Er. . .

Buying condoms from someone of the opposite sex poses a problem for only 24 percent of us, and surprisingly, there isn't much of a difference based on gender. Our guess is that not only have condom advertisers finally succeeded in their campaigns, but it's practically a necessity that you overcome whatever reluctance you might feel. Better to be safe than sorry!

Those most reluctant to buy condoms from the opposite sex are a study in contrasts, as shown by the following profile:

BASHFUL MEN	BASHFUL WOMEN
Mostly 18–29	Mostly 30–54
Right-handed	Left-handed
Long hair	Short hair
Overweight	Underweight
Tall	Short
Little body hair	Lots of body hair
No kids	Lots of kids
Earn $25,000+	Earn $25,000+
High-school-educated	College-educated

Have You Ever Had Sex in Your Parents' Home While They Were in the House?

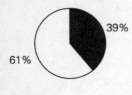

39%

61%

☐ YES
■ NO

Nearly two-thirds (61 percent) of us have had sex in our parents' home while they were in the house. It's amazing how courageous the American public can be in times like these!

Young men 18-to-29 (75 percent) and women 30-to-54 (67 percent) are the most apt to perform this daring deed.

The fearless women who tempted fate in their parents' home are right-handed, short-haired, and earn under $25,000 a year. They are tall and slender, and they are mothers.

The equally intrepid men have the same profile as the women, except that they are in the higher income bracket and they tell us they are slightly overweight.

Have You Ever Had Sex in Your Parents' Bed?

	% YES	% NO
% TOTAL SURVEYED	40	60
MEN	44	56
18–29	66	34
30–54	37	63
55+	36	64
WOMEN	35	65
18–29	50	50
30–54	38	62
55+	20	80

Do Those Old Fogies Still Have Sex? Well, If They're Not Using Their Bed . . . We'll Make Use of It!

The 18-to-29 set has been very active in their parents' beds. 66 percent of the men and 50 percent of the women have tried Mom and Dad's bed—and we don't mean as a trampoline.

It could be just a manifestation of a somewhat belated teenage rebellion—but remember that this is also the age group *least* likely to be intruded upon (22 percent of men; 27 percent of women), so that could be why they have no qualms!

Neither do the moneymakers! Those making over $25,000 are 16 percent more likely to dare this dangerous terrain than their counterparts.

Overall, however, 60 percent of Americans won't go near their parents' bed—proving that to most, it's still a "no-no."

Do Men Lift the Toilet Seat with Their Hand, Foot, or Not at All When Using a Public Bathroom?

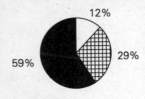

12%

59%

29%

■ HAND
⊞ FOOT
☐ NOT AT ALL

Is there a proper etiquette with regard to toilet-seat lifting? It would appear to depend totally on individual preference.

12 percent of the men ignore etiquette—if there *is* any—since they don't bother to lift the seat at all. 29 percent demonstrate a quasi-etiquette, doing it with their feet, and the remaining 59 percent actually use their hands.

25 percent of left-handed men do nothing at all, as compared with 10 percent of right-handers.

While Wearing Jockey Shorts, Do Men Pee Through the Fly-Hole, Over the Top, or Under the Leg?

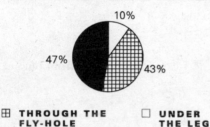

10%

47%

43%

⊞ **THROUGH THE FLY-HOLE**

☐ **UNDER THE LEG**

■ **OVER THE TOP**

Preferences may vary, but across it all the under-the-leg misters are nowhere near the favorites. And the mode of preference *does* differ depending on age: 50 percent of men 55 and over clearly like the fly-hole, while 67 percent of the younger men prefer over the top.

Those that are under-the-leg acrobats tend to be left-handed, high-school-educated individuals who make over $25,000. The exception to this rule? One of the authors, who is a right-handed senior citizen with a college degree, and who is decidedly lazy.

Have You Ever Made Love In . . . ?

We provided a short list of places where people could and do make love. Thank heavens the answers were exactly alike for both sexes when it came to the favorites and the not-so-favored. The *favorites* in rank order were:

88 percent on the floor
86 percent in the living room
82 percent in the shower

The *least* likely places to make love, chosen from our list, were as follows:

50 percent in the kitchen
38 percent on a table
36 percent in public

Have You Ever Made Love in Your Place of Business?

	% YES	% NO
MEN	**30**	**70**
18–29	23	77
30–54	38	62
55+	27	73
WOMEN	**29**	**71**
18–29	19	81
30–54	34	66
55+	35	65

I Love My Job, As Well As Love on My Job!

Just about one-third (30 percent) of Americans make love at their places of business. Both men (30 percent) and women (29 percent) are equally likely to have done it. Yet the majority still appear to be chicken.

Men aged 30-to-54, and all women 30 and over, are most likely to be the frisky employees who run the risk of getting caught in the fax room. These fearless individuals are likely to possess the following characteristics:

MEN: Earn under $25,000, college-educated, right-handed, long-haired, underweight, short in height, and lots of kids.

WOMEN: Earn $25,000+, college-educated, left-handed, long-haired, a bit overweight, very tall, and many children.

Where Is the Most Unusual Place You Have Ever Made Love?

If you thought you had an exclusive on those private, semi-private, or not so private places, check out the list provided. These unusual places were cited by *less than* 2 percent of the population. This, in effect, makes them the *"really unusual places."* They are listed in no particular order, although our personal favorite is the response that tells us that "the most unusual place I have ever made love is . . . Topeka, Kansas!"

10,000 feet up in the Sierra Nevada mountains
Bareback on a horse
Forklift
Attic
Bus
Mountain cablecar
Library
Hospital bathroom
Topeka, Kansas
747 bathroom
Platform of 35th floor— by a window cleaner
Conveyer belt
Art gallery
IBM corporate headquarters lobby

Indian reservation
Tack house
In a cemetery
School
Golf course
On top of a refrigerator
"In my wife's office with her co-worker"
A walk-in cooler
Pool table
A department store
In a church pew
St. Croix on beach in midday
Strawberry patch
Steps of a nursing home
Taxi backseat

Apple orchard
Playground at night
Rowboat
Public swing set

On flour sacks in a
   warehouse
On a Jet Ski
Behind a church

The *most frequently* cited of the "unusual places" are listed below, in rank order.

PERCENTAGES

Toilet seat	39
Swimming pool	22
Elevator	17
Camping tent	14
Beauty parlor	12
Picnic table	11
Spa	10
Rock concert	8
Tanning bed	6
Doctor's office	5
Church	3
In a tree	3

Have You Ever Watched an XXX-Rated Video at Home?

21%	16%	27%
79%	84%	73%
TOTAL	♂	♀

☐ YES
■ NO

Does it surprise anyone that 79 percent of the Americans surveyed told us that they have watched XXX-rated videos at home? And the percentages of viewership are extremely high across all genders, ages, incomes, jobs, and educational fields.

Apparently it's "the thing" for younger men and older women to do, with 98 and 84 percent, respectively, reporting engaging in this activity. In other words, XXX-rated videos at home are definitely an integral part of Americana in the 90s!

Among Those Who Watch XXX-Rated Videos at Home: Do You Make Love Before, During, or After Watching?

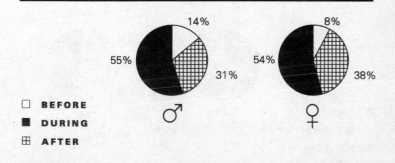

BEFORE
DURING
AFTER

A seeming oddity of these answers is that the $25,000+ group prefers making love *after* the movie, while the under-$25,000 group definitely prefers doing it *during* the movie.

The most unusual groups must be the 14 percent of men and 8 percent of women who tell us that they make love *before* the movie. Perhaps they just have a high sex drive and make love many times during the day. This group's profile is basically the same across both genders. Left-handed, they have short hair, lots of body hair, and are childless. The men report being shorter than average, while the women are taller and claim to weigh more.

Among Those Who Watch XXX-Rated Videos at Home: Do You, Your Mate, or Both Buy or Rent XXX-Rated Videos?

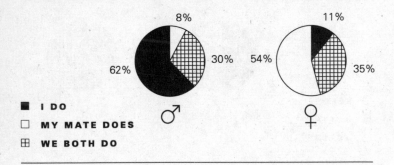

8%   11%

62%   30%   54%   35%

♂   ♀

■ I DO
□ MY MATE DOES
⊞ WE BOTH DO

In this category, the women stay clear of going it alone. Only 11 percent of women will venture into a video store to make the selection alone.

The most adventurous of these timid females? 27 percent of the 30-to-54 age group will take a deep breath . . . and plunge forward. It helps, though, to be accompanied by a partner. 35 percent of women are eager to help with the selection if their mate is right there beside them. Otherwise, it's still "a man's job" in the selection of XXX-rated materials.

The "go it alone, brave women" are college-educated and earn less than $25,000. Tall and right-handed, they have no kids and are looking forward to a wonderful evening with their partners.

Have You Ever Taken Videos/Snapshots of Your Mate in the Nude?

Among Those Who Have, Have You Ever Shown Them to Anyone?

	YES	NO	YES, I'VE SHOWN THEM
% MEN	**39**	**61**	**21**
18–29	22	78	50
30–54	46	54	9
55+	46	54	22
% WOMEN	**34**	**66**	**28**
18–29	22	78	60
30–54	33	67	17
55+	44	56	18

X-Rated America

Appearing in the buff before a mate's camera seems to please both sexes, with 39 percent of the men and 34 percent of women admitting to such a photographic venture.

The photographers are more likely to be *men* 30 and older. Slightly fewer females acknowledged taking *au naturel* pictures of their mates, but more of them showed the shots to friends than did the men.

Note: 40 percent of the respondents who had not yet taken nude pictures of their mates reported that they really would like to do so. 58 percent of these were men and 42 percent were women.

Demographics

PARTICIPANTS IN our survey came from a broad cross section of Americans and represented all the 50 states.

The following highlight some of the respondents' demographics.

53 percent are male and 47 percent are female.

Employment

89 percent of the men are employed: 81 percent full-time and 8 percent part-time.

10 percent of the men are retired.

 1 percent of the men are unemployed.

80 percent of the women are employed: 63 percent full-time and 17 percent part-time.

 6 percent of the women are retired.

14 percent of the women are unemployed.

Age

The average age of the respondents to our survey is 39 years old.

PRESENCE OF CHILDREN

58 percent of respondents have children—16 percent have one child, 50 percent have two children, 26 percent have three children, and 8 percent have four or more.

INCOME

The average income of those who responded to our survey is $42,600 a year.

EDUCATION

28 percent have completed high school or less.

52 percent are college graduates.

20 percent have postgraduate degrees.

HANDEDNESS

12 percent of our respondents are left-handed; of that, 16 percent are men and 8 percent are women.

LONG OR SHORT HAIR

15 percent of men have long hair, while 46 percent of women have long hair.

85 percent of men have short hair, while 54 percent of women have short hair.

WEIGHT

4 percent of men and 10 percent of women feel that they are underweight.

63 percent of men and 52 percent of women feel that they are average.

33 percent of men and 38 percent of women feel that they are overweight.

HEIGHT

6 percent of men and 22 percent of women feel that they are short.

53 percent of men and 45 percent of women feel that they are of average height

41 percent of men and 33 percent of women feel that they are tall.

LOOKS

3 percent of men and 2 percent of women feel that they are ugly.

44 percent of men and 45 percent of women feel that they are average looking.

53 percent of men and 53 percent of women feel that they are good looking.

INTELLIGENCE

1 percent of men and 0 percent of women believe they are below average in intelligence.

23 percent of men and 29 percent of women believe they are average.

76 percent of men and 71 percent of women believe they are above average.

BODY HAIR

12 percent of men and 28 percent of women have only a little body hair.

55 percent of men and 52 percent of women have what they think is average body hair.

33 percent of men and 20 percent of women declare they have excessive body hair.

RACE

3 percent of men and 4 percent of women in the sample are African Americans.

2 percent of men and 2 percent of women in the sample are Native Americans.

2 percent of men and 2 percent of women in the sample are Asian Americans.

8 percent of men and 12 percent of women in the sample are Hispanic Americans.

5 percent of men and 7 percent of women in the sample are of other races.

80 percent of men and 73 percent of women in the sample are Caucasians.

About the Authors

MEL PORETZ has been creative in a number of fields. In addition to writing business-paper articles and lecturing in sales promotion, he has written children's songs and a record album. He originated, and coauthored, with Barry Sinrod, *The First Really Important Survey of American Habits*, which sparked the creation of this volume. He is also the coauthor of a series of humor books called *Sam, the Ceiling Needs Painting!* The owner of a leading promotional-fulfillment organization, he is an adjunct instructor in advertising and sales promotion at Adelphi University.

BARRY SINROD, like his coauthor, is a product of Brooklyn, New York. With Mel Poretz he wrote *The First Really Important Survey of American Habits*, a zany collection of inconsequential questions such as, "Do you ever bite your toenails?" He has been a respected leader in the marketing research community for nearly 30 years, conducting surveys for many of the leading corporations, and is the coauthor of *The Baby Name Personality Survey* with Bruce Lansky. A lifelong New York Giants football fan, he claims to be the only coauthor of two recent books who has had the good fortune to be at both New York Giants Super Bowl victories. He and his wife, Shelly, have three children and two grandchildren.